To Ejima,
With Love,

Robert Trainer MD

www.robertrainermd.com

A DOCTOR'S GUIDE TO WEALTH

A Systematic Approach to Accumulating Wealth

Robert E. Rainer, MD

iUniverse, Inc.
New York   Bloomington

A Doctor's Guide to Wealth

A Systematic Approach to Accumulating Wealth

iUniverse books may be ordered through booksellers or by contacting:

iUniverse
1663 Liberty Drive
Bloomington, IN 47403
www.iuniverse.com
1-800-Authors (1-800-288-4677)

Because of the dynamic nature of the Internet, any Web addresses or links contained in this book may have changed since publication and may no longer be valid. The views expressed in this work are solely those of the author and do not necessarily reflect the views of the publisher, and the publisher hereby disclaims any responsibility for them.

ISBN:978-0-595-52980-3 (pbk)
ISBN: 978-0-595-63488-0 (cloth)
ISBN: 978-0-595-63033-2 (ebk)

Printed in the United States of America

iUniverse rev. date: 11/24/2008

Contents

Acknowledgements

I would like to express my love and gratitude to my wife, Priti, for providing a source of inspiration to allow my dreams to become a reality.

Introduction

Whatever your inspiration to become a physician, for all practical purposes, you have embarked on a lifelong mission to heal. Many physicians elect to devote their time toward research and development. Others choose to enter the world of academia. Clinical practice, typically, is the choice by most. However, the decision to become a physician often dictates that you have a sound foundation of how to operate and manage a business. Nonetheless, medical schools generally avoid the topic of business. As a result, medical students often graduate from medical school with little or no training in the business realm. For most physicians, where does the knowledge of business, in fact, originate?

The intent of this book is to provide a service. It is a descriptive narrative of the enduring process to initiate, operate, and manage a successful medical practice. It sequentially outlines an analytical process to improve mind, body, and spirit while providing a strategy for financial success. Furthermore, this book outlines the fundamental principles of wealth acquisition. The medical practice that I founded, own, and currently operate is called

MyPregnancyPlace. It is a rapidly expanding medical group currently grossing in excess of 2.5 million dollars per year, with profits, on average, increasing 30 percent annually.

There are countless challenges in the medical field today. Medical reimbursements are declining while overhead costs are soaring. However, this book provides a blueprint not only for how to establish the fundamentals of a sound medical practice but also the psychological, philosophical, spiritual, and practical approach to formulating one. Furthermore, these very same basic business principles can be applied not only to the medical field but also to virtually any imaginable business model. Hence, in simple terms, this book serves as a manual for living. It outlines a pathway to wealth while also improving mind, body, and spirit. Attaining true wealth involves maintaining mental, spiritual, and physical balance while cultivating a financial portfolio.

Additionally, this book is a descriptive protocol as to how to accumulate wealth while practicing medicine. It provides a methodical process of attaining financial success while at the same time cultivating a private medical practice with an appreciable patient volume. The proper marketing campaign, emotional mind-set, and spiritual philosophy are all key elements of a successful medical practice. These very same principles, properly applied, along with passion and the desire for success, collectively serve as the cornerstone for greatness.

PART I

THE MIND

❧ *CHAPTER 1* ☙
Desire

Desire

Desire is a measure of passion to succeed. Desire is a crucial ingredient in the effort to attain greatness and/or monetary wealth. As we define wealth, we must first establish the basic principles by which wealth is measured. Wealth is equivalent to affluence. The word affluence is a derivative of the root word "affluere." In basic terms, 'affluere' means 'to flow.' Hence, wealth or affluence by any measure is equal to the magnitude of flow. In today's society, we measure wealth by current financial standards. Many would consider a person who has a billion dollars in liquid assets to be wealthy, while others may consider that having only a million dollars is an indication of wealth.

Although my medical practice, MyPregnancyPlace, grosses millions in the single digits annually and has allowed me to accumulate a real estate fortune in the double-digit millions, wealth in the context of this book will be defined as establishing a patient flow. Any successful medical practice, in its most basic form, is a flow of patients. The larger the practice, the higher the volume of patient flow.

Desire is a key element to accumulating wealth and establishing affluence. Monetary wealth does not occur by accident. It is not a random phenomenon. Wealth requires effort. Furthermore, it requires planning and energy. In order to create a medical practice of high volume, one must passionately feel the desire and the will to make this vision a reality. The desire must be an obsession. The desire must first be visualized on a subconscious level. A subconscious vision then becomes part of our higher level of consciousness when we write down our thoughts. This is the beginning of creation. Creativity is the tool for all things that ultimately exist. As a physician, if your goal is to attain wealth, then you must see yourself as wealthy. Furthermore, you must see yourself as the physician that you ultimately desire to be. You, as a doctor, are in a unique position. Physicians, by their education and training alone, have put themselves in a very specified niche. A medical doctorate degree in itself is an immediately marketable commodity. The title of physician followed by the initials MD is a declaration of proclaimed expertise. Not only are physicians licensed to practice medicine, but they are designated experts in their fields. Hence, it is important that a physician maintain and project the role of expert. As an expert or attending physician, you do not look for reassurance and accolades from fellow members of the medical community. Clearly, this element is very important, because in order for patients to seek refuge, care, and comfort from your services, it is important that you project these ideals. Wealth and affluence are all part of the same. A large patient flow or a large practice is, in effect, wealth. Visualize yourself at its helm, and in time it will be. Houses, cars, and other tangible symbols of wealth will also subsequently follow. Desire wealth, apply energy to its creation, and universal law demands that it will come to fruition.

⬥ *CHAPTER 2* ⬦
Discipline Is the Answer

Discipline Is the Answer

"Look to your left. Look to your right.

One of those people will not be here at the end of your four years here in medical school." These are very sobering words to a group of people who have only known academic success their entire lives. How could a professor so blatantly dismiss such a large percentage of the class as destined to fail before the race even begins? We are in a race. We may not like it, and may do our best to deny it, but from birth, we are hurled into this constant competition to absorb information thrown at us. Those who accept the challenge and adjust their attitudes and mind-sets are ultimately winners. The many who believe that they can somehow outwit the system and bypass the time and energy required to absorb the information needed to reach milestones will ultimately succumb as the losers. Anyone who is described as a winner, by any sense of the word, at one time or another has utilized discipline to achieve his or her goals. But what is discipline? Discipline, in its most basic sense, is essentially an exercise in obsessive behavior patterns fueled by a particular motive. In short, it is a sort of self-imposed abuse.

Discipline's very essence remains consistent with the proverbial phrase, "no pain, no gain." Many of us are motivated by fear on some level: fear of failure, fear of ridicule, fear of God, fear of hell, fear of starvation, fear of bodily harm, or fear of death. Any one or more of the aforementioned often serves as the catalyst to motivate discipline on some level. Embracing discipline and thus performing tasks obsessively will secondarily allay anxiety and dismiss the feared outcome from becoming a possible reality.

Discipline is either self imposed or thrust upon you against your will. School, the armed services, or jail—these are not really the most glamorous assortment of choices, but in a nutshell, we all have only one choice of the three. Something extraordinary happens after we have managed to isolate ourselves in any given discipline, and we begin to enjoy the task at hand. A chosen few become the elite of their chosen domain. Enjoying a task at hand involves integrating a spiritual energy that allows one to eclipse and surpass all others. Winners often enjoy what they do. However, it is more than likely that a substantial amount of time was invested before a true payoff was noted. Nothing comes easily. Let us assume that, of the given choices of disciplines, intellectual growth is your chosen pursuit. This is possibly the wisest choice. But how do we grow intellectually? Do we converse with those who appear to be wise? Intellectual growth is attained by continuous infusion of information in order to stand out among your peers. It is unlikely that the quantity of information needed to stand out among your peers will be gained by conversation alone. Repetition and memorization of written material are the hallmarks of intellectual growth. Initially, consolidate the material to be ingested. Read the material once. Read the material again, highlighting particular key points. Lastly, commit to memory the highlighted material. Facts are committed to memory only when you are able to recite a given piece of information three times in identical fashion. This obviously takes time. Hence, the greater the compulsion utilized to follow this pattern of intellectual growth, the stronger the likelihood of prevailing over colleagues when examined. My personal fear of failure and potential subsequent ridicule was a strong motivating stimulus to push my energy to its limits while in medical school. I refused to be the one on the left or right who "did not make it."

One of those other guys would be the one who could not rise to the occasion, but by no means would it be me. Fortunately for me, it was one of those other guys who did not make it. But I cannot and will not ever commend myself as being smarter or more gifted than any of my colleagues. If anything, I was simply more paranoid than my less successful schoolmates.

Before one decides to enroll in an academic pursuit, the idea of being more intelligent or less intelligent than one's colleagues must be discarded. Academic success is entirely a function of time and energy invested. The students who are able to commit the most facts to memory are the winners, plain and simple. Studying without committing facts to memory is inefficient. Hence, in order to study in an efficient manner, facts must be committed to memory. Doing so requires energy.

Medical school, therefore, ultimately measures students who actively memorize as compared to students who do not. Medical school may also manifest the despair associated with failure. One memory of my medical school experience illustrates this very point.

There was a muffled voice emanating from the wall of the adjacent apartment.

"You're stupid! You're lazy! Nobody likes you!" I turned to my girlfriend with a perplexed look. "Who was that?" I asked.

"Oh, that's Sheila, talking to herself. I think she's failing microbiology," my girlfriend replied in an indifferent tone.

Sheila was my girlfriend's neighbor in an apartment complex largely occupied by medical students. My girlfriend was a second-year medical student who had an excellent ability to focus on the correct material at the right time with the proper amount of energy. Needless to say, she was doing very well academically. Sheila, on the other hand, was a second-year medical student with a bachelor's degree in biochemistry from the University of California, Berkeley. Clearly, Sheila was having some difficulty. Toward the end of the semester, my girlfriend informed me that Sheila had in fact, failed microbiology. Being that I was a first year medical student, there was a strong chance that Sheila would be in my microbiology course again the following year. Medical school may award you a second chance but absolutely no further opportunities if you fail a third time.

As microscopes were issued on the first day of microbiology, I noted that Sheila had been assigned to sit exactly opposite me. She nervously adjusted the focus on her microscope as she mumbled inaudible words. Another classmate sitting across from me gave me a smirk and a raised eyebrow as if to say, "Oh boy, we got a real nut job here." But for some reason, I really felt sorry for Sheila. She was a smart girl. She had graduated from UC Berkeley, truly a stellar accomplishment. Maybe she only needed to apply herself differently. Later that evening, I saw Sheila in the library. She seemed to have the study gear properly arranged, with a highlighter in her right hand and a bag of chips scattered carelessly on the left.

"I'm not looking forward to this micro nonsense," I said in a conversational tone.

She looked up and replied, "Oh, me neither. You're in my class, aren't you?"

"Yeah, I'm Bobby. Nice to meet you," I said with a smile as I gently shook her hand.

"Nice to meet you. I'm Sheila. Actually, I failed micro. That's why I'm in your class taking it now."

I was amazed that she admitted failure with such sureness. I felt that I would have fallen apart uttering that one sentence if the roles were reversed.

"Wow, I've heard horror stories about micro. I'm just hoping to get through it," I said in an empathizing gesture.

In actuality, my girlfriend had informed me that microbiology was probably most suited for me since it was very visual. But it was never considered academic etiquette to share with colleagues feelings of certainty, especially while conversing with a victim of that same course.

"But you'll probably crush micro this time since you've seen it before," I said in a supportive tone.

"I'd better. Because if I fail it, I'm kicked out of medical school," she replied in a nonchalant voice.

Did she say kicked out? Talk about pressure. She was living my nightmare. Back against the wall—fail a test and you are out! My God, not only did I feel an adrenaline surge for a predicament that did not even pertain to me, but I also made it my duty to include her in my prayers that evening.

I harnessed my theatrical skills to calmly say "You'll be fine."

But for some reason, I was not so sure. Two weeks passed, and our first microbiology examination of the semester was upon us.

An examination always appeared to be like a caged animal waiting for its prey on the dreadful test day. The students filed into the classroom in a systematic manner. I held my freshly sharpened number two pencils in one hand and a bag of M&M's candy in the other. (Studies clearly show that glucose surges while taking exams help to improve performance.) I adjusted my microscope and arranged items neatly before me, as images of different classes of bacteria danced in my mind. I was ready. Sheila then rushed into the classroom. She was late and appeared disheveled. Her hair was disorganized, and she was blatantly talking to herself. All caring aside, I was hoping that her incessant conversations with herself did not distract my concentration. At this point, it was every man for himself. Fortunately, she settled down, and her talking ceased. Midway through the examination, Sheila began to quietly whisper. The professor approached her and whispered into her ear. Again, she was quiet.

As we pushed forward during the examination, I heard Sheila softly whimpering as she supported her head with her hand. I looked up as if to alert the professor that a student was in distress. The professor walked to our table, softly said inaudible words into Sheila's ear, and gently escorted her out of the room with a supportive arm around her shoulder. Sheila failed microbiology again. Medical school administrators, true to protocol, dismissed her from the School of Medicine. I felt bad. Not only did I feel bad for Sheila, but the reality of true trauma encountered by students who experienced her kind of nightmare was ever so clear. I was not immune. If I decreased my energy one notch, her nightmare could be my reality as well.

Two months passed, and the end of the academic semester was quickly approaching. As I sat in the lecture hall, deciphering and writing facts as they escaped the lecturer's mouth, I noticed a student walking down the lecture hall walkway and taking a seat midway in the auditorium.

The classmate next to me whispered, "Can you believe it? That's Sheila. She's so bugged out she's still coming to class."

Sheila continued to come to lecture for the next month, despite the fact that she had been dismissed from medical school nearly three months earlier. At that point, it became blatantly clear that any level of success has an associated cohort of losers. Be a victor at all costs because living as a loser may prove unacceptable. Sheila's fate remains undetermined to this day.

Many people are motivated by responding to negative impulses. Clearly these thoughts of impending failure or doom can compel individuals to astonishing accomplishments. But, undoubtedly, repetitive negative reinforcement will ultimately have detrimental effects. In order to be great, you must believe in your greatness. We all have within us an unleashed potential. But let us focus on the two world orders that universal law follows.

As individuals, we have a choice whether or not to believe in God. We may be believers or nonbelievers. If we believe, we are afforded unlimited potential. If we know that we are guided, loved, and directed, then we will aspire to unimaginable heights. Believers are receptors to God's universal energy. Believers have no doubt. They are motivated by forces beyond their being. If we choose to follow positive universal order, then there is nothing that we cannot do. Believe it. Cultivate it. Many of us may refer to this as our spirituality. If spirituality is a term that confers depth and meaning, then, by all means, use it. Spirituality allows us to serve as a receptor to God's positive universal forces. Understanding and accepting the belief that God loves, guides, and directs is paramount in optimizing the strength of universal forces.

Conversely, along with a positive universal order, so too exists a negative one. Those who choose to ingest the inverted order of envy, hate, doubt, and fear, fall victim to Satan's praise. Know no fear, feel no hate, and dismiss doubt and envy—for these are voices of negative universal order.

Although you may not be the Son of God, we are all children of God. If you are of the Christian faith, then you believe that only Jesus had absolute faith. No doubt existed since his faith in his Father was absolute. But through Jesus's words, he conveyed to his disciples that he who has faith will follow in his path. Hence, Jesus's power was his absolute faith. We may never achieve absolute faith. But it is the pursuit and cultivation of our faith that allows us to serve as better receptors of positive universal order. Believe in God, and believe that God loves you, guides you, and directs you, and with Him you cannot go wrong. Repeat this four times a day, and ultimately you will believe.

CHAPTER 3
The Subconscious Mind

The Subconscious Mind

The human brain possesses infinite wisdom. As we make note of our five tangible senses—taste, hearing, touch, smell, and sight—we must realize that our brains perform a multitude of tasks in the absence of conscious thought. Hence, there is a level of brain activity that is beyond our awareness. It is beyond what we recognize as everyday brain function. Our subconscious minds are not entirely understood, but they are perpetually active. Our subconscious minds empower our imaginations to orchestrate our reality. They manifest our visions. Nonetheless, our subconscious minds are fueled by the instructions that they receive. The commands fed to our subconscious minds, will, in time, materialize as a physical equivalent. Hence, we must write down what we wish to become. Documenting our goals allows the subconscious mind to process and digest the information. Nonetheless, the subconscious mind requires constant attention. Therefore, we must incessantly program the subconscious mind with the key instructions in order to fulfill our destinies. This incessant programming is synonymous to a compulsion or desire.

Forrest Gump is a wonderful movie that highlights the wonderful capacity that an obsessive nature affords. Although Forrest Gump possessed an inferior IQ at best, his obsessive nature led him to excel in every endeavor that he pursued. The obvious message here is that a persistent obsession will, in time, manifest a desired result. If you truly desire wealth, then make wealth your passion. Feed your subconscious mind the material input that it needs to fulfill its mission. The enormity of the mind will then manage the remaining details. Our hearts beat in the absence of thought. Clearly, our minds have the capacity to take us far beyond our physical reality. However, it is important that we continuously infuse the proper ingredients to allow our subconscious minds to unveil our visions.

That being said, we must make a concerted effort never to implant seeds of negativity. Negative impulses such as fear and anger negate the productive function of the subconscious mind. Fear and anger are counterproductive. Jesus Christ instructed us to love. He stated that love is the answer. Why is this so? Love creates flow. We are attracted to it. We pursue it. It is the passion that compels us as human beings. Love is the frequency that positively resonates with human emotion. Love can move mountains. Furthermore, love negates the actions of fear and anger and serves as the premise by which all creativity resides. A mind that utilizes love as its fundamental narrator has no boundaries. Designed in the image of our creator, our capabilities are limitless. Our potentials are endless. Our success resides with Jesus's one simple instruction: "Love all."

⊂ध *CHAPTER 4* ৯০

Electrical Physics Parallels Business Dynamics

Electrical Physics Parallels Business Dynamics

In the late nineteenth century, a German-born physicist, Georg Ohm, discovered the fundamental equation of electrical physics. Ohm stated that the basic premise of electron flow in an electrical circuit was a function of this equation:

$$I = V \times \frac{1}{R}$$

The variables of the equation are as follows:

I = electrical current flow
V = voltage or potential difference
R = electrical resistance

The function of this equation calculates the magnitude of electrical flow given the amount of voltage and resistance in an electrical circuit. Contemporary economists draw parallels between business dynamics and the movement of electrons in an electrical circuit. Hence, the dynamic of business revenue growth directly correlates to Ohm's equation of electrical physics.

Thus, simply put, human consumer behavior mimics the movement of electrons in an electrical circuit.

If we utilize Ohm's law of electrical flow, we can correlate this to business dynamics. Hence, I hereby deem the final equation as *Rainer's Postulate* of Consumer Dynamics in a Business Model:

$$I = D \times \frac{1}{C}$$

I = customer flow (analogous to electrical current)

D = demand of service (analogous to voltage)

C = cost of service or product (analogous to resistance)

Customer flow is at its greatest if product demand is high and product cost is low. Cost, in this case, is equivalent to resistance relative to the electrical circuit. Demand is analogous to voltage potential. Lastly, customer flow is equivalent to electrical current.

Furthermore, we can further define resistance of business flow by including quality of service. Hence, our equation defining the dynamic of business yields:

$$I = D \times \frac{1}{\frac{1}{Quality} \times C}$$

I = customer flow

D = demand of service

C = cost of service or product

Q = quality of service

Further computation yields the final equation or *Rainer's Postulate:*

$$I = Q \times D \times \frac{1}{C}$$

(Rainer's Postulate)

Rainer's Postulate computes customer flow (I) as maximal if product quality (Q) and demand (D) are high and cost (C) is minimal. In the final equation of *Rainer's Postulate*, of particular note, is that the quality of service (Q) is an integral variable determining customer flow (I). This intuitively follows because business success is often a function of service quality, which invariably determines business viability or demise. If we analyze our equation further, we note that business flow (I) is equivalent to quality (Q), if cost (C) and demand (D) are equal.

$(I = Q$ if $C = D)$

Hence, business flow, or magnitude of service (I), is equivalent to quality of service (Q), given that demand (D) and cost (C) are equal.

In a profound sense, this mathematical equation supports the premise that a sound business with a large customer base is effectively built upon quality of service and customer satisfaction. If we extrapolate this further, we can note that quality, caring, and love are all one of the same. In essence, business flow (I) equals (Q) quality of service. $(I = Q)$. Can we not further state that business flow is equivalent to the expressed love for its customers? Flow equals love. Jesus stated this thousands of years ago.

In many respects, physicians fundamentally provide the same service. With insurance coverage being the norm and demand of service effectively a relative constant, the magnitude of patient flow is merely a factor measured by the quality of care and/or compassion given to each patient. Thus, the hallmark of a successful medical practice is integrating love into the overall context while providing quality up-to-date services.

Many have capitalized on the basic premise of the equation, Flow equals Love $(I = Q)$. Many leaders, including evangelical, spiritual, and musical (Joel Osteen, Mahatma Gandhi, Martin Luther King, and Bob Marley) have all embraced and utilized love's power in amassing extraordinarily large followings. Today's preachers, ministers, and musicians have filled stadium-sized arenas by dispensing love on a large scale. Love is power. Thus, in many respects, it is the fundamental resource that we all need.

PART II

THE BODY

☙ CHAPTER 5 ❧
Alcohol Appeases Peasants

Alcohol Appeases Peasants

What makes us decide to have a drink? Is it the taste? Most of us will agree that alcoholic beverages have a characteristically repulsive taste, similar to the first attempt to inhale a cigarette. Is your body telling you something by this initial reaction? But despite these early bodily warning signs, many fall prey to the depths of alcohol addiction. Many lives, careers, and morales have been destroyed by alcohol abuse.

Alcohol is a central nervous system depressant. It inhibits proper neural function at toxic levels. But toxic levels can only be achieved once the liver, our body's filter, is completely overwhelmed. When the liver can no longer filter alcohol, and our kidneys lag behind in their effort to excrete it, then alcohol intoxication ensues. Nerves become disabled, thoughts disorganized, and inebriation follows. The Bible clearly states that alcohol is the drink of peasants. Peasants may need to be periodically desensitized to their poor state of existence. Hence, alcohol may have served as a mode of maintaining compliance among the masses. However, alcohol has no place for the consumption by aristocracy and kings.

Euphoria—a state of well-being and a sense of spiritual self— is perpetuated by our body's release of endorphins. Endorphins are our body's natural morphine and they are also the cause of a "runner's high," and possibly the inspiration for an inventor's vision and a philosopher's wisdom. They dull the realization of physical pain. Endorphins spiritually connect our body's self to a higher plane. Alcohol inhibits endorphin release.

In the complete absence of endorphin production, pain is accentuated, our mind's ability to rationalize is altered, and creativity is diminished. Life becomes a painful experience. Is this not the vice to allow us to become spiritually disengaged?

Aging occurs when the body's resourcefulness approaches depletion. Cells divide to create new tissue in order to allow proper organ function. A newly divided cell requires fresh protein and an abundant water supply. Considering that our physical being is generally composed entirely of a 70 percent water and a 30 percent protein blend, compromising either of the two ingredients is detrimental to our well-being. Hence, alcohol expedites the aging process because it causes the kidneys to eliminate water, and it causes our liver to discontinue protein production. Newly created cells lack essential raw materials. Aging, therefore, ensues prematurely.

Those convinced that alcohol relaxes them are possibly deprived of the benefit of meditation and prayer. Meditation and prayer are exercises that allow the mind to extinguish aberrant, irrelevant thoughts. In turn, positive thoughts may be reinforced. "God loves me, guides me, and directs me, and with Him I cannot go wrong." Repeating this to myself five times daily has allowed me to endure the rigors of medical school, build a thriving practice, and create a portfolio in excess of ten million dollars while still in my early forties. Our faith allows us to function in the spiritual plane. Alcohol severs our spiritual essence. A personal childhood memory vividly paints this picture.

He spoke freely and uninhibitedly. My grandfather worked for thirty seven years at U.S. Steel. Did he complete high school? Did it matter? He worked hard, raised his family, and drank heavily at the end of a work day. The following morning, he repeated the process. I truly loved my grandfather. He spoke openly and shared stories that a nine year old child would marvel at. Perhaps it was merely the conversation of mentor to child that appealed to me most. He would sit in an upright chair on the backyard patio. The night crickets would play their soothing melodies. My grandfather would hold a small glass containing a pungent, gold colored drink. The summer heat would melt the ice. His weathered, swollen hand would encase the glass. He would stare out into the night as if he visualized an object far away, amid the darkness. His voice was calm, almost poetic, and he would recount distant visions of his own childhood. I grabbed onto every word that came from his mouth—the wisdom of so many years shared with the inexperience of youthful ears.

"Bob," he would say, "when I was a boy your age, we didn't have all the things that you have. I'd get up in the morning, real early. First, I would chop wood. It be cold, you know. And my mother wasn't goin' to have no cold house with no wood in the woodstove. And I would walk outside in the cold. Sometimes I would put tape on my shoes to cover the holes. All the kids did that. We were all poor, so no one felt ashamed 'cause none of us had no money. Then I'd feed the chickens. I did this every morning before I walked to school. Me and my sister walked to school. That was a long walk too. Every year we got a new pair of shoes. We began to sing,

'I've got shoes ... You've got shoes ... All God's children got shoes. When we get to heaven, goin' to put on those shoes and goin' to walk all over God's heaven ... heaven ... all God's children goin' to heaven."

❦ *CHAPTER 6* ❧
The Body

The Body

As you visualize your course for greatness, it is imperative that you employ a defined regimen to improve your body. Improving your physical well-being means establishing good habits. Daily exercise is essential. Exercise should consist of jogging for a minimum of twenty-five minutes with an elevation of heart rate to at least 140 beats per minute. This level of exercise intensity will stimulate the production of brain endorphins. Brain endorphins, in turn, are an internal source of creativity that enhance your engagement with God.

Good habits yield positive results, and they should be reinforced. However, it is important to note that a viable course for greatness exists only in the absence of addiction. Many, unfortunately, succumb to the ills of addiction with vices such as cigarettes, alcohol, and drugs.

However, heroin addiction, one of the most horrific addictions of all, is the chemical link to the Antichrist. Synthetic endorphins such as heroin cause the body to cease production of its own internal stores of endorphin. By doing so, heroin use secondarily serves as the toxin to disengage one's link with God. Additionally, alcohol, which also suppresses brain endorphin release, dulls mental acuity.

Many of us are aware of chemical and substance addiction. But, food overconsumption should also have a prominent place on the list of addictions.

Nearly 50 percent of Americans are overweight. Obesity is the source of a multitude of pathological diagnoses such as diabetes, osteoarthritis, hypertension, cardiovascular disease, cerebral vascular disease, cancer, heart attacks, and strokes. In simple terms, excess food kills.

The food industry, in its own overzealous effort to market its products, has excelled in the effort to convey the joy of food consumption. However, it is up to each individual to employ restraint. Fad diets and exercise gimmicks have little to no value. We must accept the fact that weight gain is a function of an excess of calories ingested relative to the amount of calories burned. Furthermore, mathematical analysis also reveals that one pound of body fat equals 3,500 calories. Therefore, we would need to spend five hours on a treadmill burning seven hundred calories per hour to lose one pound. Clearly, this is a rather daunting task.

But, unfortunately, many of us continue to be seduced with the all so familiar fad diets promising unrealistic weight reductions with minimal effort.

For a moment, let us observe the effect of food on a cellular level. In fact, this level of scrutiny may assist us in our efforts to restrain ourselves from overindulging. Pharmaceutical companies make billions selling drugs that lower cholesterol. But is a lower cholesterol value really a solution to an improper diet? Even more importantly, will a lower cholesterol value, in of itself, increase longevity? It is

A Doctor's Guide to Wealth

well established that there is both good and bad cholesterol. Good cholesterol is defined as High Density Lipoproteins (HDL) and bad cholesterol as Low Density Lipoproteins (LDL). Cholesterol is, among its other roles, a transport system for different foodstuffs throughout our blood stream. Large fat molecules are transported by LDL, and smaller, healthy complex carbohydrates are carried via HDL.

Imagine a diet consisting of healthful fruits and vegetables. Furthermore, let us assume that the complex carbohydrates in these foods are analogous to small, thin women. Now imagine a high fat diet consisting of ice cream and bacon, which secondarily produces large fat particles requiring transport. These fat particles are analogous to sumo wrestlers. The small thin women (i.e. complex carbohydrates), are carried in highly mobile minivans. These swift moving minivans are comparable to the HDL in circulation.

Conversely, the large sumo wrestlers require large city buses (i.e. LDL) to travel throughout the vascular system. As the large LDL particles (comparable to city buses) maneuver through the circulatory system, they indiscriminately crash into the vessel walls along the vascular highway. Comparatively, the HDL molecules, analogous to the smaller minivans, move through the vessel without injury. Consequently, once the vessel wall suffers an injury from the large LDL cholesterol particles, construction crews are recruited to repair the damage. These repair "crews" consisting of fibroblasts and platelets, aggressively patch the vessel wall injury. This site of vessel wall repair is called an atherosclerotic plaque. Repeated vessel wall damage with subsequent repair enlarges the atherosclerotic plaque and, in time, narrows the vessel lumen.

An enlarging atherosclerotic plaque, over time, may ultimately cause complete vessel occlusion, resulting in a subsequent heart attack or stroke. Although this is a rather simple analogy, unfortunately, this disease process results in the death of millions of people each year. Furthermore, studies continue to show a direct link between severity of atherosclerosis and high levels of LDL.

Notwithstanding, your body is your temple, and in order for your mind and spirit to work in harmony, your body must perform optimally. Optimal performance of your body starts with maintaining your ideal weight. Reaching your ideal weight, however, requires that you be cognizant of your basal metabolic rate. Basal Metabolic Rate (BMR) is the average amount of calories your body consumes on a daily basis. The formula to calculate BMR is as follows:

Women:

BMR = 655 + (4.35 × weight in pounds) + (4.7 × height in inches) – (4.7 × age in years)

Men:

BMR = 66 + (6.23 × weight in pounds) + (12.7 × height in inches) – (6.8 × age in years)

Once you are aware of your daily caloric requirement, it is imperative that you not consume in excess of this figure.

Body Mass Index (BMI) is another calculated figure that equates to a person's relative ideal weight. The body mass index is a figure that equals a person's weight in kilograms divided by a person's height in meters squared. Hence, BMI equals kilograms divided by meters squared.

$$BMI = \frac{weight\,(kg)}{height\,(m)^2}$$

or

$$BMI = \frac{weight\,(lbs) \times 703}{height\,(in)^2}$$

A BMI from 18 to 25 is normal. A BMI from 25 to 30 is overweight. A BMI greater than 30 is obese. Hence, through proper nutrition and exercise, it is important to reach and maintain the proper range of 18 to 25.

In your pursuit of intellectual and spiritual growth you must strive additionally for physical excellence. As you establish yourself as a leader you must exhibit a distinct command of your physical well-being. This is particularly important not only for your personal health but also throughout your course to heal others.

Invariably, as a physician it is important to stress the significance of exercise. Routine exercise facilitates harmony between mind and body. But it is important to clearly define exercise. The significant majority of us walk from point A to point B, but is this justified truly as exercise? In order for physiological gains to occur from exercise, a certain amount of stress must be placed on the body. In fact, physical gains from exercise are the body's reaction to the stress placed upon it. Studies continue to support superior health benefits from a vigorous treadmill exercise regimen. Furthermore, jogging, a weight bearing exercise, far exceeds the health benefits of walking, which is not a weight-bearing exercise. Each day I spend twenty-five minutes jogging on a treadmill at a rate of six miles per hour. This regimen is sufficient to attain a heart rate greater than 140 beats per minute. Studies have shown this to be the heart rate threshold needed to yield improvements in the HDL and LDL profile. Additionally, bone density and cardiovascular status likewise improve at this level of exercise intensity.

(Of course, consult with your physician prior to beginning a new exercise regimen.)

This twenty-five minute daily run also provides an opportune time to pray. Prayer while exercising allows mental and spiritual cleansing. The mind and the body become one, and mental clarity is attained. Hence, physical well-being is essential to attain true harmony. When the body suffers from internal conflict it is not at ease. This is the basis for the term, "dis-ease." This internal bodily conflict or "dis-ease" requires energy and, subsequently is a diversion from spiritual focus.

Vitamins are important elements that assure proper function of the body's mechanisms.

Vitamins are organic compounds that assist our enzymes in their basic mechanistic functions. Additionally, vitamins with antioxidants are extremely valuable, as we will later discuss.

Our bodies consist of more than 70 percent water. Although the sun is a natural source of vitamin D, its ultraviolet rays can cause bodily harm. Ultraviolet rays can split the water molecule, H_2O, into its two basic components. Subdivided, water becomes a hydroxyl group (OH) and a hydrogen ion (H). The hydrogen ion is a charged particle with one unpaired electron. This hydrogen ion, with its charged particle, is called a "free radical." Antioxidants are of benefit because they bind and secondarily eliminate excess free radicals in circulation. Free radicals in abundance can cause an enormous amount of destruction throughout the body. Free radicals bind to cellular DNA and thus interfere with cell division. Furthermore, free radicals can also bind to DNA and cause genetic mutations, which may even lead to cancer. Hence, the aging process is hastened by an excess of circulating free radicals. So, clearly, ultraviolet rays with their secondary production of free radicals can indeed be harmful. The body's defense mechanism in response to excessive ultraviolet rays is the production of melanin or skin pigment. Hence, a tan is the body defending itself from a disproportionate amount of harmful ultraviolet rays. Extremely fair skinned people, unable to produce significant amounts of melanin, show more vulnerability to the sun's harmful and destructive ultraviolet rays. Thus, routinely avoiding excessive sunlight and ingesting antioxidants are two simple strategies that slow the aging process.

If we were to evaluate the progress of medicine during the past one hundred years, invariably antibiotics would be considered one of medicine's finest achievements. Antibiotics, in their ability to thwart and treat serious bacterial infections, have been one of medicine's greatest triumphs. However, to date, our ability to combat viruses is nominal at best. Stem cell research, along with DNA sequencing, offers enormous promise in production of cellular tissue and possible replacement of organ systems. Research in this area may indeed improve longevity and also improve quality of life. However, in the meantime, focusing on proper diet, avoidance of alcohol, and proper nutrition remain the mainstay for good health.

As we focus on accumulation of wealth, we must embrace the notion that the premise of wealth acquisition is based on love for others. Wealth is merely a by-product of the power of love to establish a flow. A body in conflict or not at ease lacks harmony. Hence, a body in disharmony is at odds in achieving harmony with others. Thus, the very notion of a physician healing others must begin with healing from within. Thus, our wellness sets the stage and image for others to emulate. We must therefore avoid obesity at all costs.

In all fairness, we cannot assume that obesity is equivalent to poor self esteem. People may be confident despite being obese. However, obesity is a predisposing factor that, if left unchecked, will ultimately lead to internal disharmony and conflict. Obesity is the premise for disease. Additionally, its very existence is the manifestation of habitual poor habits. Thus, thwarting the affliction of obesity is largely a resolute commitment to regular exercise. Make exercise a daily part of your routine. Enjoy playing a sport, and make it your directive to eat healthy foods such as fruits and vegetables and foods low in calories. As a physician, you are a teacher as well as a healer. Healing others begins with healing from within.

PART III

THE SPIRIT

∽ CHAPTER 7 ∾
FAITH

Faith

I believe in God. I believe in Christ. For me, these are the fundamentals of faith. Faith is a very strong element in ultimately acquiring wealth. As we persevere in life's journey, physical, intellectual, and spiritual pursuits are all components of a worthy struggle. Faith, however, is the spiritual element that should motivate us each and every day. But, first, we must ask ourselves, What is our faith and how important is it for us? For, without faith, there is no truth. Without truth, there is no purpose.

Faith is the cornerstone of purpose. It is the ultimate motive behind acts of goodness.

My day begins with prayer. As I recite the Lord's Prayer, I feel connected with God. When I finish the Lord's Prayer, I ask Jesus Christ for direction. I ask Jesus Christ to allow me to give love to those whom I see. I ask Jesus to allow me to give love and to heal those whom I touch. And I ask Jesus Christ to touch those whom I speak to with his words. Faith is a connection to a higher power.

Faith is regulated by the production of endorphins in the brain. Hence, exercise, meditation, prayer, and laughter are manners by which we may produce brain endorphins. Conversely, alcohol suppresses brain endorphin levels. Hence, it is important, if not essential, to avoid alcohol in your quest for greatness. As we focus on faith, it is important to understand its magnitude and power. Jesus's message while on Earth was clear. He instructed us to love all. Not only were we instructed to love those who loved us, but, more importantly, Jesus instructed us to love our enemies. This is a rather enormous undertaking, given that clearly we should not expect anything in return from loving our enemies. However, Christ instructs us to do so. How do we measure our personal faith as it involves our practice of medicine?

In addition to adherence to modern medicine's accepted standards, faith should be a fundamental element in our daily practice of medicine. It is a privilege to be labeled a healer. It is a job ordained by God. To heal with faith under the watchful eye of God is to heal with the premise of love. In its perfect form, healing is through love. A physician who loves his patients promotes well-being by initiating the cascade effect of healing. Care for a patient as if the person were your mother, sister, father, or brother. What lengths would you go to in order to guarantee that patient's survival? Undeniably, for a family member, only the best would do. Make this level of care your personal standard for all.

The human psyche gravitates toward love. It is our ultimate destiny. We seek it, and, by all practical purposes, we spend a great deal of time and energy cultivating it. Physicians cannot effectively heal while consumed with their own personal issues which clearly serves as a conflict toward accomplishing a higher purpose. If each physician, in the midst of a physical examination, said a silent prayer for the patient, then illness and pathology would, in effect, decline. Science is only beginning to uncover the power of spiritual faith in the healing process. A recent study enlightened and surprised researchers as they noted that postoperative cardiovascular patients healed more readily if they received silent prayer. Conclusively, prayer's direct link to physical well-being is a consistent finding even by today's research standards.

Wealth in medicine is attained through establishing flow. A positive bond with one patient serves as a beacon for others to follow. A routine part of the physical examination involves evaluating the eye's conjunctiva to rule out the presence of anemia. This brief moment, in the context of an overall physical examination, serves as an opportunity to express spiritual love through the eyes of Jesus Christ. Peer into the eye and silently acclaim, "I love and heal you with the strength, courage, wisdom, and power of Jesus Christ." This encapsulates the strength of spiritual healing and galvanizes your commitment to heal as a physician.

Ultimately, you heal through faith, and consequently it is your faith that inspires you to heal. As a physician, your job has purpose. It is this purpose that may serve as the cornerstone in your endeavor to attain wealth.

PART IV

THE STRATEGY

CHAPTER 8

Wealth with Real Estate

Wealth with Real Estate

This book has defined wealth as it relates to the volume of patient flow in a medical practice. Now, we must make an effort to translate wealth denoted by patient flow volume into a self-perpetuating source of capital. Real estate, by its very definition, characterizes this type of wealth. It is wealth distinguished by its nonmovable nature and documented by a deed. However, there are objective variables tied with real estate. Its value, for the most part, increases over time due to increasing inflation and increasing demand from a growing population. This phenomenon of real estate appreciation is highlighted if we envision taking a transcontinental flight across the United States. Most of the land in America as we look from the skies above, is uninhabitable. It is noted to have rugged terrain, mountains, and wetlands. Clearly, this area is unsuitable for a proper infrastructure such as electricity and running water. However, let's imagine a seven-bedroom mansion with a three-car garage. Immediately, your mind assigns value to this home. But if this same house were placed in a deserted plain in the Midwest with no running water or electricity, then this immaculate mansion would have a virtual dollar value of zero. But, of course, place this same home on a waterfront New York City, Manhattan lot, and its value skyrockets upwards of double digit millions. This example showcases the fact that real estate value is effectively 100 percent based on location. A growing population gravitates toward limited land mass, and hence real estate in this desired location appreciates in value. Given that real estate value effectively has consistent growth in specific locales, this book will only focus on real estate located in three of the most highly valued property locations in the United States: Manhattan waterfront property located along the Hudson River in Battery Park City, New York; Miami Beach, Florida; and beachfront property in Santa Monica, California. Real estate value in these three locales, by definition, will increase with time.

It is also very important to discuss the difference between personal and social value, as it pertains to real estate. Personal value is a reflection of the worth imposed by the owner and not the value assigned by a potential buyer. Value assigned by a potential buyer is defined as social value. An owner's personal attachment to a home is deemed personal value. Many homes fail to sell because the owner may have performed upgrades that have immense personal value but may have limited value to a potential buyer, i.e., limited social value. Hence, an accurate real estate appraised value is effectively based on the value of properties of closest proximity. This is termed property comparables. A property noted to have high comparables has an associated increased social value and will subsequently have a high appraisal value. Furthermore, this suggests that many potential buyers would desire to purchase the home. Thus, certified appraisers have the most significant impact on the value of any given piece of real estate. An appraiser's final monetary value placed on a home will be the bank's most important determinant when calculating a maximum mortgage. Hence, a homeowner should take precaution prior to performing numerous renovations (increasing personal value) if neighboring homes are notably depressed in value. Thus, relatively speaking, it is better to have the worst house in a great neighborhood as opposed to the best home in the worst neighborhood.

One accurate predictor of a "good neighborhood" versus a "bad neighborhood" is the median annual household income. The median annual household income is a median dollar figure of the households in a given area. If the median annual household income of a given neighborhood is 50 percent or more greater than the national median annual household income, then, by definition, the area is deemed a "good neighborhood."

Although a physician makes a comfortable income, it is imperative that this income be invested into a self perpetuating source of wealth. Real estate provides this investment opportunity. The question then becomes, "How wealthy do I choose to be?" Condominiums are excellent real estate investment opportunities. They offer secure and safe investment venues reinforced by the fact that banks willfully provide finances to purchase them. We also need not mention that the basic necessities of life, such as food and shelter, ensure that a condominium purchase would likely have a tenant eager to pay rent. Battery Park City in New York is an oasis for condominium investment. Located along the Hudson River in Manhattan, New York, property in Battery Park has steadily managed to appreciate 15 percent annually.

For our purposes, let us assume that we purchase our real estate condominium in Battery Park City, New York. Additionally, let us assume that our successful medical practice affords us a $180,000 annual investment sum. If we were to invest $180,000 per year in Battery Park City condominiums, after three years, our gross real estate investment would have a value of $4,000,000. Additionally, the net equity value of the three combined properties would total $1,800,000 with a monthly cash dividend of $1,800 per month.

These numbers come to fruition if we were to do the following. Let's say we purchase a condominium with an asking price of $1,000,000. The number one rule in real estate investment is to never pay the asking price. Instead, we offer 90 percent of the asking price which is, in effect $900,000. If our offer is the agreed price, we then must put down or pay 20 percent or $180,000 of our agreed price. We would then find it necessary to mortgage the remaining balance of $720,000. Mortgage brokers are very helpful in this regard. They secure loans utilizing various venues such as banks, private lenders, etc. Given that our intentions are to purchase this property as an investment property, an interest only loan is ideal. An interest only loan involves paying the interest of the mortgaged amount, but the loan principal remains the same over time. But an interest only loan has an advantage, given that the monthly mortgage note is typically lower and can often be offset by the rent charged to an occupying tenant. A note of caution is to avoid Adjustable Rate Mortgages (ARM). These mortgages initially begin at low monthly payments but in time may balloon to extraordinarily high monthly mortgage notes.

Our second rule of thumb in real estate investment is to make certain that our real estate cash flow remains positive. In effect, this means that the rent charged to a tenant exceeds the monthly mortgage and maintenance fees needed to pay for the condominium overhead. If we were to put this theory into practice by buying one condominium each year for a total of three consecutive years, then we would note the following: a $180,000 per year investment would total $540,000 in three years. In three years, we would own three Manhattan waterfront condominiums. Each condominium value would appreciate from $1,150,000 to $1,320,000 to $1,520,000—in effect, 15 percent annually. However, the mortgage owed on each condominium would remain fixed at $720,000. Hence, the total value of the three condominiums with a 15 percent annual appreciation after three years is $4,000,000. Additionally, our combined net equity in the three condominium properties is equivalent to $1,800,000. Hence, a $540,000 total cash investment has become a $1,800,000 cash value in a three year time frame. Overall, our annual cash investment has grown at a rate of 51 percent each year.

It is noteworthy to mention that the stock market may also serve as an excellent investment venue. Although I have placed 10 percent of my wealth portfolio primarily in Apple and Google stock shares, real estate by far is the mainstay of my investment portfolio. Notably, who could argue an annual 51 percent return of money invested utilizing real estate. Each condo purchased is, in effect, a brick in the structure of your personal wealth empire. Hence, only our imaginations can limit the size of the empire that we wish to build.

‹∞ *CHAPTER 9* ∞›

Planning and Marketing

Planning and Marketing

A great physician's practice starts with perfect planning and is executed with superior marketing. As a physician, ultimately your job is to provide a service. In fact, the quality of this service will, in time, dictate the measure of success of your practice. Medical schools spend an enormous amount of effort to enable medical students to diagnose and to apply critical thought in determining a patient's diagnosis and treatment. However, there is, in effect, no time spent addressing the ultimate question as to how to establish a medical business.

Patients will judge you. It is the subjective human nature that exists for both good and bad. Therefore, physicians must be aware of all elements by which they are judged. Is the physician's appearance clean? Is his or her lab coat exceptionally pressed and white? Is the furniture in the waiting room tasteful? An exceptional physician's practice not only answers yes to these questions but, in its extreme, makes particular note of these details. Your office is an extension of you as the physician. From decor and furniture layout to the music softly played, all are reflective of the treating physician. Therefore, it is imperative that a physician notes and takes considerable time to understand and appreciate the perspective by which the patient perceives his or her office experience.

How do you design a medical practice? Although you may ask yourself this question, for the most part, the question is already answered. As a physician, you have chosen to embark on well-charted territory. In all likelihood, there are already physicians in practice, performing and maintaining a business in your chosen specialty. In effect, it is no secret as to how these physicians currently in practice generate revenue. As medicine evolves and becomes more socialized, medical insurance companies or Health Maintenance Organizations (HMOs) often dictate reimbursement rates for medical and surgical procedures for which they will compensate. As a new physician, it is very important to obtain a list of these procedures in which HMOs typically reimburse. Become familiar with the reimbursement rates. Understand the Current Procedural Terminology (CPT) codes for your given specialty.

Undeniably, the cornerstone of every physician's practice is both the treating physician and the manner in which billed accounts are collected. Medical billing is a billion-dollar business. Furthermore, make no mistake that there are hundreds, if not thousands, of medical billing companies interested in doing business for you. However, the notion that every medical billing company has the best interests of the physician at hand is implausible. The medical billing company, depending on its size, often may disregard fine details of a particular procedure or surgery in its effort to collect funds as quickly as possible. Regardless of the manner in which a medical billing company collects revenue for a physician, never will they forgo the 8 percent commission they charge.

Because billing agencies are efficient at earning 8 percent of your hard earned revenue while at the same time downplaying the details of your hard work, then outsourcing medical billing will ultimately prove to be counterproductive. My wife performs all the medical billing in my office. I firmly believe that this fact has secured my practice's leadership status. No detail goes uncovered with my wife at the helm of the practice's medical billing. Furthermore, it's imperative that I emphasize that the success of a medical practice is only as good as the quality of service and the efficiency of its medical billing. I love my wife, but I feel her passion for success transcends our relationship as she brings a successful, detailed, and goal-oriented approach to collecting accounts receivable. Initially, as your medical practice evolves, outsourcing medical billing may prove practical, since it may decrease overhead expenses. But, in time, it is essential to perform all medical billing in-house. As a physician executes the procedures and services of his or her given specialty, be assured that your fees and reimbursements have been predetermined.

Many describe the 1970s as the golden era of medicine. Medical practitioners were reassured that they would receive justifiable compensation for the work performed. However, with the emergence of socialized medicine, justifiable compensation is a thing of the past. In 1970, a gynecological surgeon typically would earn upward of $5,000 for a five hour abdominal hysterectomy case. Today, a gynecological surgeon for the same case will earn no more than $1,100. Hence, the monetary compensation is not reflective of the time, energy, and effort for the procedure performed.

Physicians and surgeons are now forced to be businessmen and businesswomen. Their creativity and vision are essential to their business success and/or survival.

Thus, creating revenue streams is essential for fiscal survival. However, bear in mind that the 80/20 rule is always in full effect. In essence, the 80/20 rule states that 80 percent of the income is generated by only 20 percent of the revenue generators. Put another way, out of ten ideas to create revenue, only two will succeed and the remaining eight will result in dismal failure. So, for every great moneymaking idea that you have, you'd better have four other ideas in succession to improve your odds for success. Thus, generally speaking, successful people perpetually create. It is the onlooker's perception that these people are successful, since spectators tend to dismiss failures and glorify victory. Hence, perpetual creativity is the true resource of wealth.

Creative minds continuously adapt to a changing environment. We must, therefore, never allow ourselves to become complacent with an established condition. In time, all things change. This includes customer demands along with competitor status. Hence, it is imperative to implement every sound idea. Although the 80/20 rule dictates that only two of ten ideas will succeed, unfortunately, we are not privy to this outcome until we experience and risk the possibility of failure. Thus, practically speaking, success comes only to those who have managed to fail at least four times.

Medical practices survive from reimbursement revenue for established medical services and surgical procedures. Hence, it is crucial to review and comprehend the list of compensated medical procedures as it relates to your specialty. Thoroughly understand the list, for it is the lifeline by which you will survive. Certain surgical procedures that typically generate revenue from HMOs, such as a dilatation and curettage, require a relatively short amount of time to perform. However, their reimbursement rates are reasonably good. In fact, two dilatation and curettages performed within a twenty minute time span reimburses the monetary equivalent of one four hour total abdominal hysterectomy. The physician must recognize this disparity and, furthermore, must capitalize on it. Marketing for the sake of marketing has limited value. But a more important question is, How many D&C's did I perform in the previous week? Answer the question, and it will give substance to your marketing goals.

When we discuss marketing, we must realize that marketing, in its simplest form, is selling a service in print. This is particularly true for direct mail. The marketing mechanism allows the potential consumer an opportunity to visualize the product or service prior to making a purchase or committing to pay for a service. Therefore, marketing must be creative, clever, reassuring, and artistic. However, the best marketing plan will never exceed the efficacy of patient word of mouth. In fact, studies show that medical practice volume increases tenfold via patient word of mouth as opposed to any other marketing vehicle. Thus, marketing is, in effect, a tool that assists a current customer in his or her effort to verbally describe your service. There are various venues utilized to market a medical practice—radio, television, direct mail, yellow pages, and the Internet—to name a few. But in terms of marketing efficacy, imagine a relatively simple experiment. As a physician, imagine creating two marketing plans. One plan involves marketing aimed to members of a community in Hong Kong via a five-million-dollar television advertisement. The other plan involves paying a high school student to pass out paper flyers describing your medical practice located in Brooklyn, New York. In all likelihood, the student passing out flyers in front of your medical office in Brooklyn, New York, would have a higher efficacy than a multimillion-dollar ad campaign in Hong Kong.

This happens for various reasons. First, potential consumers in Hong Kong have an obvious geographic barrier in receiving your product or service. Secondly, the language obstacle may present itself as an obvious problem. And, lastly, if you are not a Chinese physician, it is very unlikely that potential consumers may feel comfortable relating to you. I give this example to illustrate the ultimate paradigm in business. Regardless of your effort to select your patient demographic, invariably, patients choose their own physician. Hence, it becomes very important from the vantage point of physicians to understand the variables by which they are chosen by their patients, prior to creating a marketing campaign.

Patients often select their physicians based on race, age, gender, nationality, perceived fund of knowledge, and compatibility. How friendly are you as a person? Are you a good listener? Are you interested in the patient's history? Patients possess a great deal of insight while evaluating you as a physician. Ultimately, their perception of the quality of your service will dictate their desire to recommend you to others. Love your patients: it is the pinnacle and greatest level of care that a physician can provide. Furthermore, it permeates every aspect of the physician-patient experience. Imagine each patient as if she were your mother or your sister. What standard of care would you provide to them?

As we market our practices, a solid rule of thumb is to measure the cost of the advertisement dollars in comparison to the amount of revenue created for any given ad. The current average reimbursement rate for an infant delivery is $2,500. Thus, let's assume that we intend to create a marketing campaign aimed at potential pregnant women with a marketing budget of $5,000. Empirically, our advertisement campaign would have to, at the very least, net two pregnant patients. This is essential, because a marketing campaign investment should, at minimum, have an equivalent revenue return.

To have a firm grasp on the demographic variables when devising a particular market campaign is extremely important. First and foremost, it is imperative to come to the realization that your established patient cohort is, in effect, the demographic that you should direct your marketing campaign towards. Pull one hundred charts from your current shelf of established patients, and write down the following objective characteristics from each medical chart: the patient's age, race, and zip code. These three variables provide a good start as to how to direct a marketing campaign.

When deciding which advertisement medium is best to use, I offer a firm and straightforward recommendation. Direct mail is the most efficacious marketing vehicle to promote a medical practice. Direct mail is a direct link to the community. A well-crafted, artistic, four-by-six-inch direct mail piece is invaluable when establishing and cultivating your medical practice. It should include photos and graphics representative of your practice, services that you provide and a photo of the physician—all of which are illustrated in an aesthetic, creative, and artistic format. InfoUSA is a company that provides nationwide mailing lists. These mailing lists are a vital resource when designing a marketing campaign. Furthermore, the mailing lists may be tailored based on specific characteristics of the targeted mail recipients. As mentioned earlier, age, race, and zip code are important variables that define perspective patients of a given medical practice. Make it your marketing commitment to mail five thousand direct mail pieces monthly to your specified population. This monthly commitment has purpose and intent. In order for your business vehicle to take flight, it must first be given enough velocity to assume lift. A well orchestrated direct mail campaign is the engine that provides velocity for your business aircraft.

Although I find it important to have a Web page representative of the medical practice, as well as ultimately a yellow page ad, the direct mail campaign will far exceed all other forms of marketing in its investment return. I think that it is important to stress that expensive forms of advertisement such as television and radio serve little to no value in an effort to expose a new and/or established medical practice. The advertisement costs in these two venues far exceed the likely investment return.

As we discuss wealth as it relates to patient flow, invariably, we must consider wealth as it relates to the possession of tangible goods. Ultimately, all wealth is relegated to real estate owned. As we yield the fruits of a successful medical practice, invariably the money generated will be invested in real estate. At some point, the owner and operator of a medical practice must own his or her office space. Undoubtedly, rented office space allows a practicing physician to decrease overhead expenses. However, be warned that the owner of the office space will always have their sights on the revenue that you generate as a physician. Henceforth, the office space owner will further adjust your monthly rent in accordance with the perceived success of your practice. Thus, a physician may fall victim to his or her own success if the landlord elects to increase office rent expenses in excess. Even worse, a physician risks possible eviction if tenant/landlord negotiations fail. Therefore, in time, it is imperative that every physician owns his or her own office space. Assuming this, researching real estate becomes paramount. Analyze existing practices in your field, and pay particular note as to their location. There is nothing unethical in moving your medical practice in close proximity to an existing competitor. However, the patient demographic of the competitor must closely resemble that of your own.

Furthermore, real estate is an important investment vehicle. The value of real estate is based on demand. It is interesting to note that a flight over the North American continent reveals a great deal of information. For the most part, the majority of the land and the territory of the United States is uninhabitable. Unfavorable terrain and nonexistent resources in some areas make it impossible to survive there. This fact reinforces the premise that the value of real estate is based entirely on location. In fact, real estate value increases in time because the increasing population demands to reside within a fixed limited space. Thus, the value of any given real estate is, in effect, based on the comparable values of the property most proximal to it. It is important to understand the value of real estate and its significance because, ultimately, it may provide a monetary refuge in a time of crisis. New York City; Miami Beach, Florida; and Santa Monica, California are three real estate locations that, with time, have all increased in value.

As you invest in real estate, the earned equity of its increasing value may serve as a financial reservoir in the event of a monetary need. Make your office your home. Own it, decorate it, and bless it with the familiarities and comforts of your existing home. Patients are an extension of you. They are your friends as well as invited guests to your home. Treat them as such. Love and luxury are both elements that contribute to your success. How you integrate these two variables into the overall context of your business will, in time, determine the magnitude of your success and ultimately your wealth. Both are powerful and equally important. Handle each with care.

❧ CHAPTER 10 ❧

Specialized Procedures

Specialized Procedures

Education is a very noble and important pursuit during a lifetime. Furthermore, if you have earned a medical doctorate, attached to it comes a certain degree of admiration and prestige. But merely earning an MD degree is often not enough. A successful medical practice requires more. The practical application of a medical doctorate degree, properly executed, may materialize into financial prosperity. Thus, it is prudent for the physician to become familiar with up-to-date and current reimbursement rates. Furthermore, understanding, acknowledging and possessing a high degree of proficiency in the most current procedures and services is of utmost importance. One case in point is as follows: In the field of gynecology, the preferred method of surgical elective sterilization was traditionally performed using a laparoscopic instrument. The laparoscope enabled a small half-inch incision to be placed on the navel to insert the laparoscope and secondarily allow the fallopian tubes to be ligated. Both patient satisfaction and reimbursement rates for this procedure were satisfactory. However, a company by the name of Conceptus manufactured a mechanism to occlude the fallopian tubes using an instrument called a hysteroscope.

The advantage of the hysteroscopic method was to allow the elective sterilization to be performed intravaginally without the need for any abdominal incisions or scars. Lastly, the reimbursement for the hysteroscopic method was nearly threefold the rate of the laparoscopic method. Overnight, the once supreme laparoscopic method fell into disfavor. The new hysteroscopic method became the accepted norm. Hence, it is the physician's obligation to become knowledgeable and competent while performing various procedures in a given field. It is important to point out, however, that not all procedures will fall into the spectrum of a given practice. Each physician must know his or her limit. Furthermore, there is no degree of dishonor in transferring a patient to a consulting physician if the patient's diagnosis falls outside of the scope of a physician's established practice.

Physician wealth is built on the premise of performing the highest volume of procedures in the shortest amount of time. There is no ignoring this simple fact. Proclaim your niche within your specialty and appoint yourself as best. It is rare, at best, that physicians bestow accolades on fellow physicians. In theory, it is truly counterproductive, because each physician is, in fact, a competitor among other associates. Thus, proclaim yourself as the greatest, and, in time, it will come to pass. For many, Muhammad Ali best exemplified this notion. For the vast majority of his career, Muhammad Ali incessantly attested that he was the greatest. Incidentally, Ali chanted his mantra, "I am the greatest," despite the fact that his critics felt otherwise. But, with time, Ali's prophecy became fact. Accordingly, many today would be hard pressed to name any other heavyweight boxing champion greater than Muhammad Ali.

Award yourself, and refrain from seeking awards, particularly from other physicians. Awards, in many respects, are often symbols bestowed upon compliant followers for performing tasks requested of them. Your mission as a leader is to create a following. In turn, this following will serve as the source of your affluence. But understand that this journey will, by no means, be free of challenge and conflict. Challenges will remain bountiful. However, each challenge should act as a mechanism to stimulate the creativity that exists within. Viewed in the proper context, challenges merely serve as seeds of opportunity.

In every aspect, your mind serves as your weapon. It should be treated and nurtured as such. Alcohol dulls mental acuity and creativity. On the other hand, exercise and moderate coffee intake stimulate mental productivity. Given that our mind is constantly active, it continuously seeks and utilizes creativity to overcome problems and challenges. Failure is, therefore, not an end result. It is merely a milestone that defines the next challenge. Thus, periodic failure validates a viable competition. In most instances, success cannot be attained without first enduring a succession of failures. These failures are mere setbacks that characterize your path to greatness. As long as the competition remains viable, you are always winning.

Creativity is often a term that we apply when our faith is utilized. Faith and prayer are the basic resources that nurture our subconscious thoughts. Ultimately, our subconscious thoughts come to fruition as we attempt to define creativity. Thus, daily prayer is our weapon to confront our challenges. Prayer is not only useful but is also very practical. Every challenge has an answer. Each answer opens the door for further opportunity.

Your creativity serves as the instrument you use to meet the demands and rigors as CEO. As you fulfill your rightful place as a company CEO, understand the following: No one will praise you. Few will thank you. But many will be inspired by you. A true leader stands alone on a mountaintop.

∾ CHAPTER 11 ∾
You Are the CEO

You Are the CEO

Given that you have decided to pursue a career in medicine, your education has served as insurance for your well-being. But establishing and maintaining a medical practice, in simple terms, means that you are the boss. You are the CEO. As the CEO of your business, success or failure rides completely on the day to day decisions that you make. Your success or failure affects all of those who place their faith and confidence in you. In fact, your employees stake their livelihood on your survival. Naturally, this should serve as your source of inspiration. Given that you have made it thus far, for the most part, there is nothing to stop you. But being a great CEO, for all practical purposes, means that you must act like a great CEO. Competitors, associates, and staff scrutinize you. They observe your mannerisms. They analyze your moods. They observe your demeanor. They even note your dress and weight. In a sense, you are the patriarch of the family. A CEO is a visionary. He or she must continuously create ideas that may generate revenue but must also accept the fact that not all ideas will succeed. Furthermore, he feels the climate in which his business currently resides and predicts the forecast for the upcoming day. To accurately predict upcoming events, you must be aware of every imaginable element of your business.

Revenue intake versus expense output defines growth or decline. The CEO, therefore, must have a firm grasp on every revenue source that the business generates and must furthermore create venues that warrant financial merit.

To increase marketing focus on one business facet while de-emphasizing another is pivotal to the role of CEO. Hence, understanding the financial vital signs of the business is crucial.

Additionally, the CEO has a responsibility to perpetuate the business philosophy, which must be embraced by the entire work force. Without fail every month, I hold a staff meeting. During the staff meeting, I discuss certain elements of the business. Business objectives and goals are stated. Our standing relative to our competitors is also noted. Furthermore, staff members who are performing exceptionally well are pointed out. A staff meeting always ends with reaffirmation of the positive spiritual and integrity commitment that is shared by myself and employees alike. We love our patients, and we love one another. This reaffirmation of the business philosophy is very important. It gives each staff member definition and purpose. I cannot express enough the importance of the staff sharing the mind-set of the CEO who employs them. In many respects, each employee is an extension of his or her boss. Hence, each patient's experience, to a large extent, is based on the interaction with both physician and staff alike. Additionally, the CEO must know the strengths and weaknesses of each and every employee. All employees are not the same. Thus, the jobs that are delegated to them should also vary. It is the CEO's job to interpret the distinctive capacity of each staff member and thus decide what project best suits him or her. It is also very important to note that excellence should be praised. In addition to verbal acknowledgement, monetary awards should also be given to those who show superior performance. Awards as such should be displayed to other employees in order to motivate them and to furthermore allow an enhanced feeling of self worth by the employee on the receiving end. Conversely, employees who perform poorly should be admonished. But it is important to do this in private in order to preserve overall morale.

Communicate openly with the staff. They provide a wonderful resource of information, sharing insights about the efficacy of marketing campaigns to overall patient satisfaction. Every year, I take my entire staff, along with their significant others, on a ski trip vacation. On the vacation, we lease a large seven-bedroom home, cook wonderful meals, play video games, and, most of all, have a great time on the ski slopes. It is a fun, healthy time for all of us. But it also facilitates and cements the existing fundamental group bond. The trip, in itself, communicates to the staff that the business is indeed fiscally healthy and furthermore has positive financial projections. Additionally, it serves as positive reinforcement, rewarding the team for work well done throughout the year. Lastly, it is a golden opportunity to reinforce and express business ideals and philosophy.

As a physician, you have secured your future by obtaining an education. Now it is prudent that you further secure your future by embracing the proper business fundamentals and principles. Your focus, cheer, will, and determination set the tone and help to navigate the course of your business destiny. Love others, and you will receive love in return. Your business will ascend to phenomenal heights as a mere result of implementing Jesus's directives.

CHAPTER 12
Love is Luxury

Love is Luxury

Humans have a basic necessity for food and shelter. But all humans are drawn to luxury. But what is luxury? How do we define it? Clearly, luxury, in its simplest form, is great attention to detail. Additionally, one can envision being surrounded by an assortment of valuables. But in a broader context, luxury requires energy and effort. Many familiar brands, such as the Ritz Carlton hotel chain, are associated with luxury. Furthermore, the Ritz Carlton is known to be associated with superior service. In essence, no detail is overlooked. Providing luxury or superior quality of service is also very important in a medical capacity.

The business of medicine has evolved into two categorical business models. Capitation and fee for service are the models by which most medical companies are run. The capitation business model involves providing medical service for a specified group of individuals in a given population. The health providers for this predetermined group, in turn, are provided a preset amount of money to care for this cohort of patients. At the end of the fiscal year, remaining funds after providing medical care for the given population is deemed business profit. Clearly, this business model of medicine contains inherent flaws. The health provider, under the capitation medical system, would be encouraged to withhold medical care to save revenue and thereby increase annual profits. The quality of care afforded by the patient invariably suffers. On the other hand, the fee for service business model provides another means of administering health care for a given population. The fee for service model entails providing medical care as it is deemed necessary. Furthermore, each medical service provided by the health care provider is billed, and a subsequent fee is collected. Hence, the greater the number of medical services that are provided, the larger amount of fees collected and, hence, the greater amount of business profit. The fee for service medical model exemplifies medicine at its best. Under the fee for service medical model, a delay of diagnosis and/or insufficient care are far less likely. Under this system, the healthcare provider is encouraged to perform routine patient evaluations.

I am a huge proponent of the fee for service medical model, and I believe it is an essential aspect of a successful medical practice. Utilizing a fee for service model enables a physician to provide a superior quality of service. But wealth as it relates to a medical practice is built on establishing patient flow and increasing volume over time. A large patient flow cannot sustain on the grounds of mediocrity. From its conception, an exceptional medical practice must exude excellence. Thus, a medical practice who's goal is to attain excellence must utilize the fee for service paradigm.

I reside in a Ritz Carlton waterfront condominium. The condominium's appraised value in the year 2008 was 3 million dollars. Although my home is a symbol of business triumph, in a greater sense it represents the collective love and support that

I receive from a passionate patient following. I love my patients, and they, in turn, love me. Consequently, this exchange enables me to purchase real estate of exceptional value. Patients are our loyal followers, and they, in turn, deserve the absolute best. Luxury must therefore be the gold standard of service.

It is unfortunate that today's medical climate is extremely litigious. With this being the case, a handful of patients may have an adversarial attitude toward their physician. Physicians must not only be naïve to this particular patient disposition but also take the necessary precautions to avoid an air of indifference or disdain by both physician and staff alike. Nonetheless, an adversarial patient is entitled to proper medical care. If the adversarial patient poses a conflict and creates a climate of disharmony for the vast number of compliant patients, then it is certainly ethical for the physician to transfer the patient to an associate practitioner. However, the compliant patient in need of medical care is indeed the staple of your medical practice. That patient is the key element to your greatness and success. Accordingly, this patient should receive a great deal of warmth and compassion during his or her office visit.

The corporation that I founded in the year 2000 is MyPregnancyPlace.com. It has become one of the largest and most successful obstetric and gynecological practices in Brooklyn, New York. The company motto, "MyPregnancyPlace loves you," communicates a direct message to the members of the Brooklyn community that I service.

Medical care received at MyPregnancyPlace is exemplified by superior quality, attention to detail, and love for all patients.

Each prenatal patient at MyPregnancyPlace receives a free body massage at the Ritz Carlton Hotel and Residence in Battery Park City, New York. As mentioned earlier, I reside at the Ritz Carlton building in Battery Park, New York. Thus, each of my prenatal patients is indeed a welcomed guest to my home. This sends a profound message to the patient population at large. Regardless of a patient's background, race, or socioeconomic level, she is entitled to the highest quality and standard of medical service. Furthermore, luxury is an integral part of this experience.

Be generous. Generosity is rewarded ten fold in the overall scheme. We want money; therefore, we give money. It is a universal law and universal order that dictates what you give ultimately determines what you will receive. This spiritual doctrine is also referred to as karma.

In its most basic sense, money is merely a symbol. It is a note of appreciation—a nonverbal gesture of thanks for services rendered or products received. How many people do you currently service? Ask yourself this question and the answer will provide an accurate assessment of your current monetary status. How many people do you desire to service? The answer to this question provides a yardstick to the magnitude of wealth that you may ultimately achieve. Thus, the magnitude of your wealth is inherently tied to the magnitude of service that you provide. We may service our communities, the nation, or the world, but each level of service equates to a particular caliber of wealth. For instance, providing Pap smears for an entire community may produce a moderate amount of wealth. Secondly, providing a Human Papilloma Virus (HPV) vaccine for the nation can, in turn, provide a greater degree of wealth. Lastly, providing a Human Immunodeficiency Virus (HIV) vaccine for the world may provide extraordinary wealth.

Hence, wealth parallels the level or magnitude of service that we provide. But however we measure our degree of wealth, it all begins with providing service to one individual. After providing medical care to a patient, my greatest reward of highest inspirational value occurs when a patient says "Dr. Rainer, I sent my sister and my mother to you, and we all absolutely love you.

You are our doctor forever."

PART V

CONCLUSION

CHAPTER 13

Politics and Medicine

Politics and Medicine

Universal healthcare is currently a hot topic in today's political arena. Many newly elected politicians promise low healthcare costs for each and every citizen. But these proposed healthcare initiatives come with a likely tradeoff. Quality of care invariably suffers. Furthermore, many attempts to lower the costs of healthcare involve adopting a capitation system and secondarily curtailing physicians' salaries via stringent contractual arrangements. Although many physicians express reluctance in operating their own practices in fear of exorbitant overhead costs and increasing malpractice premiums, one fact remains clear. Physician autonomy and freedom rests upon the utilization of a fee-for-service medical system. Physicians should not be seduced into the mainstay healthcare workforce because of the fear of facing the challenges of operating one's own enterprise. If all physicians were to commit to a contractual salary position, then the bureaucratic screws would tighten, and negotiating leverage would vanish. Physicians must preserve the entrepreneurial spirit of a free-market system. The time honored tradition of our specialty and possibly our liberty may be at stake.

In regard to the topic of capitation versus fee for service medical models, I would like to highlight a key issue. Many physicians utilizing the fee-for-service medical model in a private practice setting have established contractual agreements with large corporate HMOs. Furthermore, the HMO performs its physician re-credentialing process annually in order to renew any preexisting contract. A strong note of caution is in order. Never become complacent and "assume" that your physician-HMO contract will be renewed on an automatic basis. HMOs may terminate a physician from its panel at any time with no discernable explanation. A nonrenewal of a physician-HMO contract "without cause" speaks volumes regarding an HMOs bottom line. Beefy Corporate HMO profits prevail as priority number one and patient welfare and physician economic security arrive at a distant second. If you have the misfortune of receiving an HMO contract nonrenewal letter, fight back! Send a return letter to the HMO requesting a retraction of intent of contract nonrenewal. Additionally, forward a copy of the letter to your state governor. If your response from the HMO is unfavorable then initiate litigation proceedings. As physicians, the Hippocratic Oath obligates us to serve our patients with beneficence. This code of conduct prevails in the office, hospital, operating room, and negotiating forums with unscrupulous HMOs.

There are few remaining points that I feel deserve firm emphasis. Obtain a post office box. A post office box allows flexibility in the physical location of your office. Additionally, it insures that the incoming mail insurance check revenue stream is tamper proof.

Of course, pay your taxes. It is absolutely pointless to amass significant wealth only to have it dismantled due to nonpayment of taxes. I employ a large Manhattan accounting firm to file my annual tax returns. Marks, Paneth, and Shron is a reputable accounting firm that, each year, submits superior quality tax returns. Furthermore, in the event of an IRS audit, they fully represent your business and personal interests. Having the security of a meticulously detailed and accurate tax return is well worth the added expense. Your job is to create new financial sources. Let others labor the details of your path.

Lastly, when the opportunity lends itself, give back to the community. So often, people have enormous expectations of government in solving every dilemma of modern society. But, it is the private sector that needs to take initiative in order to confront the challenges that face our communities. Five years ago, I began an annual scholarship called the Dr. Robert Rainer SAT Achievement Award. The scholarship is a $1,000 cash award given to the high school senior student with the highest SAT (Scholastic Aptitude Test) score. The award is given to a graduating senior student at George Westinghouse High School in Brooklyn, New York. George Westinghouse High School is a predominantly African American high school in an underserved area of Brooklyn. While the broader goal of the scholarship was to improve SAT scores and inspire a greater number of students to attend college, several changes were noted to occur after instituting the scholarship. First, the median SAT score of graduating senior students climbed sharply. Secondly, the number of students taking the SAT examination increased. This, subsequently, led to more students continuing on to pursue a college degree. But what I found extremely delightful was that students embraced the profound message that others cared about their future. This in of itself was priceless.

While money serves as the motivating stimulus to achieve an end result, this example illustrates the benefit of serving others. It is undeniable that attaining financial success is an achievement worthy of recognition. However, lending assistance to those less fortunate bestows honor in amassing fortunes.

❧ *CHAPTER 14* ❧
Final Thoughts

Final Thoughts

I was once asked who I intended to target with this book. I really felt that I had no clear definitive answer. Established physicians could clearly profit from the book's content. If you are a business owner in pursuit of greater profits, then this book may also serve you. If you are a student in search of direction in life, this book may serve you. But don't we all need goals—maintaining mental, spiritual, and physical balance while pursuing financial prosperity? Shouldn't we each have a sense of purpose? My path to success is not a series of chance events. Granted, I am worth millions, but not billions of dollars like Bill Gates, for example. Additionally, I did not create Google or ebay. However, I have pursued a viable, fruitful, and exciting course in life that has, in every respect, paid off very well. Adhering to a consistent simple regimen of reading, running, and praying while serving and loving thy neighbor, in many respects, defines our lifelong mission. The reason that my journey warrants documentation is because the entire course can be reproduced. My success is not based on chance encounters with influential people or from exploiting extraordinary God-given talents. My success is a testimony of hard work, persistence, discipline, and faith. Therefore, no one particular demographic is best suited to read this book. If you wish to be healthy, then this book may serve you. If you desire wealth, then execute the aforementioned principles. If you would like to reinforce your faith, then believe, and it will be so. We all wish to reach our greatest potential. In doing so, we must think big. Delegate whenever possible. Fill economic voids when the opportunity presents itself. Love always, for it is the universal frequency that positively resonates with mankind. No dream is too big. But failure to execute a vision relegates it to remain a dream. Embrace the book's content in its entirety. Integrate each component into your life wherever possible. But never lose sight of the big picture. In one form or another, we are all meant to serve each other. Figure out your particular passion, and the rest will unravel on its own. But above all, let the destination inspire you, but always enjoy the journey. God bless.

About the Author

Robert E. Rainer, MD, is a graduate of the University Of Maryland School of Medicine. He completed his residency training in obstetrics and gynecology in 1995 and shortly afterward established his medical practice, MyPregnancyPlace. Dr. Rainer's practice flourished and is now a leading OB/GYN practice in New York City. With annual profits exceeding 2.5 million dollars, Dr. Rainer has built a premier medical practice and a real estate empire valued at over 10 million dollars. Learn the insightful secrets that have guided Dr. Rainer to financial prosperity while still in his forties.

Web site: www.mypregnancyplace.com